coffee

INDULGENCES

coffee
INDULGENCES

SUSANNAH BLAKE

PHOTOGRAPHY BY MARTIN BRIGDALE

RYLAND
PETERS
& SMALL

LONDON NEW YORK

First published in the
United Kingdom in 2007
by Ryland Peters & Small
20–21 Jockey's Fields
London WC1R 4BW

www.rylandpeters.com

10 9 8 7 6 5 4 3 2 1

ISBN: 978 1 84597 468 8

A CIP record for this book
is available from the British Library.

Printed in China

Notes

• All spoon measurements are level,
unless otherwise specified.

• Ovens should be preheated to the
specified temperature. Recipes in
this book were tested using a regular
oven. If using a fan-assisted oven,
follow the manufacturer's instructions
for adjusting temperatures.

• All eggs are medium, unless
otherwise specified. Recipes
containing raw or partially cooked
egg should not be served to the very
young, very old, anyone with a
compromised immune system or
pregnant women.

• It is recommended that the milk
used for these recipes be full-fat, as
this will give a better result.

• The water used to make coffee
should be just off the boil. This is
what is meant by 'just-boiled water'
in the ingredients throughout the book.
Pouring boiling water over coffee
grounds makes it bitter and impairs
the flavour.

Senior Designer Amy Trombat
Editor Céline Hughes
Production Gemma Moules
Publishing Director Alison Starling

Prop Stylist Helen Trent
Food Stylist Bridget Sargeson
Assistant Food Stylist Stella Sargeson
Index Hilary Bird

CONTENTS

COFFEE

– made from ground roasted coffee beans – is loved and drunk the world over and there is a wealth of ways of making and serving it. Whether it's infusing the grounds in boiling water, forcing steam through them to obtain a strong, dark liquor, brewing in a pot with sugar or leaving to drip through a filter, everyone has their own traditions and preferences. And serving it is open to just as many options, whether it's strong and black, rich and milky, foamy and frothy, piping hot or icy cold.

In Italy and Spain, a strong cup of coffee can be drunk on the way to work, while standing at a bar. In Vienna or Paris, you might linger over a cup of coffee at a table in a coffee house or café. In Vietnam, where the French left their legacy of coffee-drinking, you will find people sitting in cafés drinking the Vietnamese take on *café au lait* made with sweet condensed milk, while in Turkey, the fine grounds are brewed in boiling water and the resulting unfiltered coffee is drunk very sweet and black.

But coffee isn't just for enjoying as a drink; it's the perfect flavouring too. It provides a natural partnership with numerous other flavourings and ingredients, such as vanilla, chocolate, nuts, toffee and caramel, praline, nougat and warm spices such as cinnamon and cardamom. Dark and bitter or subtly elusive, the taste of coffee is perfect in pastries, mousses, custards, sauces, creamy desserts, refreshing ices, cookies and cakes, and hot and cold drinks.

And the ways of injecting that essential coffee flavour are as diverse as the possible pairings and vehicles. A strongly brewed coffee or a shot or two of espresso might be perfect for making drinks, granitas, ice creams and custards, but for cakes and cookies where you need an intense hit of coffee without the volume of liquid, good-quality instant coffee dissolved in a small amount of just-boiled water is the ideal thing. Roasted or chocolate-covered coffee beans can be folded into batters or ice creams and mousses rather like the ubiquitous chocolate chip for an entirely different type of coffee hit. Coffee liqueurs, such as Kahlúa and Tia Maria, provide an intense, sweet coffee kick and are great for adding flavour on their own, or paired with another coffee flavouring, such as espresso.

When buying coffee, there is usually a vast choice. The beans can be divided into two types – arabica and robusta – of which the arabica has a more refined taste. Columbia, Kenya, Java and Costa Rica, for example, refer to the country of origin. Brazil is the world's largest producer, but it is grown across Central and South America, Africa, Asia and South-East Asia, and the taste and aroma varies from region to region and even from estate to estate according to soil, climate etc. However, Jamaica (from the Blue Mountain estates) is widely considered to be of excellent quality.

There are numerous ways of brewing coffee, but it can be divided mainly into three for the purposes of this book: espresso, cafetière (or press pot) and filter (or drip).

Espresso is made by forcing steam through coffee grounds to extract a small quantity of very dark, strong coffee. Machines are available, but the simplest (and cheapest) method is with an espresso pot that can be used on the stove top. The pot unscrews to reveal a bottom chamber, which is filled with cold water. A perforated receptacle is then filled with coffee grounds and fitted on top of the lower chamber and the jug with a feeder tube from the receptacle below is screwed on top. The pot is then heated until the water boils and bubbles through the grounds to produce a strong, dark brew in the upper pot.

The cafetière is filled with coffee grounds (about 1 tablespoon for a regular cup of coffee, but more for a strong brew), then very hot but not quite boiling water (92–96°C is considered perfect) is poured over the top and left to brew for about 5 minutes. The sieved plunger attached to the lid can then be pressed down to separate the coffee from the grounds.

Filter coffee can be made in one of several ways, but the simplest method is through a paper filter into a jug below, although you can also get filters for individual cups. Coffee grounds are placed in the filter, then just-boiled water poured over the top and left to drip through the grounds. Filter coffee machines often have a hot plate under the jug to keep the coffee warm.

However you like your coffee, and whatever your tastes in sweet treats, you'll find something in *Coffee Indulgences* to give you that inimitable coffee hit.

cakes, cookies and afternoon treats

COFFEE, MACADAMIA AND
WHITE CHOCOLATE CHUNK COOKIES

These big, fat, chunky, chewy cookies are subtly flavoured with coffee and studded with chunks of white chocolate and macadamia nuts. Serve with coffee, tea or an ice-cold glass of milk.

115 g butter, at room temperature

200 g caster sugar

1 egg

1 tablespoon instant coffee dissolved in 1½ tablespoons just-boiled water

100 g macadamia nuts

100 g white chocolate, roughly chopped

100 g self-raising flour

100 g plain flour

two baking sheets, greased

makes about 15 cookies

Preheat the oven to 190°C (375°F) Gas 5.

Beat together the butter and sugar until creamy, then beat in the egg, followed by the coffee. Stir in the macadamia nuts and chocolate and mix together.

Combine the flours and sift over the cookie mixture, then stir until thoroughly combined.

Drop heaped tablespoonfuls of the mixture on to the baking sheets, spacing them well apart. Bake for about 10 minutes until pale golden and slightly puffed up.

Leave the cookies to firm up for a few minutes, then transfer to a wire rack to cool.

COFFEE BEAN AND CHERRY BISCOTTI

These long, elegant, crisp Italian cookies studded with chocolate-covered coffee beans and dried cherries are the perfect treat for coffee lovers to enjoy with their mid-morning brew.

85 g plain flour

85 g self-raising flour

60 g polenta

85 g caster sugar

2 eggs

1 teaspoon vanilla extract

50 g dried cherries

50 g chocolate-covered coffee beans

30 g blanched almonds

a baking sheet, greased

makes about 20 biscotti

Preheat the oven to 160°C (325°F) Gas 3.

Sift together the plain and self-raising flours, polenta and sugar into a large bowl and make a well in the centre.

Beat together the eggs and vanilla extract and pour into the dry ingredients. Add the cherries, coffee beans and almonds and stir. Knead gently until the mixture comes together into a sticky dough.

Shape the dough into a log about 20 x 10 x 2 cm and put on the prepared baking sheet. Bake for about 30 minutes until golden.

Remove from the oven (leaving the oven on) and leave to cool for about 5 minutes, then transfer to a chopping board and cut into slices 7 mm–1 cm thick. Arrange the slices on the baking sheet and bake for a further 15–20 minutes, turning halfway through, until crisp and golden.

Remove from the oven, transfer to a wire rack and leave to cool.

COFFEE AND WALNUT MACAROONS

Coffee and walnut is a winning combination and divine in these golden,
chewy macaroons. They have a wonderfully rich, bitter-sweet flavour
and gooey, crunchy, sticky texture – perfect with a cup of coffee.

115 g walnut pieces

115 g caster sugar

2 egg whites

1 teaspoon instant coffee dissolved
in 1 teaspoon just-boiled water

12 walnut halves

rice paper

makes 12 macaroons

Preheat the oven to 180°C (350°F) Gas 4. Cut out twelve 7.5-cm
rounds of rice paper and arrange on two baking sheets, spaced
well apart.

Put the walnut pieces and sugar in a food processor and process
until finely ground. Set aside.

Put the egg whites in a clean, grease-free bowl and whisk until
they stand in stiff peaks.

Add the coffee, then sprinkle over a couple of tablespoonfuls of the
ground nut mixture and fold in. Continue folding in the ground
nut mixture a few tablespoonfuls at a time.

Spoon round dollops of the mixture into the centre of each piece
of rice paper (leaving a little space around the edge to allow the
mixture to spread out during cooking). Top each one with a walnut
half and bake for 12–15 minutes until golden brown.

Carefully transfer to a wire rack and leave to cool.

SQUIDGY COFFEE BARS

These wonderfully rich, moist bars studded with chocolate chips, hazelnuts and sticky fudge
fall somewhere between a brownie and a cookie. They're divine served slightly warm
and freshly baked, but they're pretty sensational served cold as well.

150 g butter, at room temperature

100 g caster sugar

100 g light soft brown sugar

1 tablespoon instant coffee dissolved
in 1 tablespoon just-boiled water

1 large egg

225 g self-raising flour

60 g dark chocolate chips

70 g blanched hazelnuts,
roughly chopped

70 g fudge, roughly chopped

*a 20-cm square cake tin, greased
and lined with greaseproof paper*

makes 12 bars

Preheat the oven to 190°C (375°F) Gas 5.

Beat together the butter and caster and brown sugars until
smooth and creamy. Beat in the coffee, followed by the egg.
Sift over the flour and fold in, then fold in the chocolate chips,
hazelnuts and fudge.

Spoon the mixture into the prepared cake tin, spread out evenly
and bake for about 25 minutes until golden and risen. Leave to
cool in the tin for about 5 minutes before cutting into 12 bars.
Leave to cool for a little longer in the tin, then carefully peel off
the greaseproof paper.

COFFEE, PECAN AND MAPLE CAKE

A twist on the classic coffee and walnut cake, this light, golden sponge
is rich with the flavour of toasted pecans and filled with a sweet,
buttery frosting with a hint of coffee and maple syrup.

180 g butter, at room temperature

180 g caster sugar

3 eggs

180 g self-raising flour

2 teaspoons instant coffee dissolved
in 1 tablespoon just-boiled water

60 g pecans, roughly chopped

frosting

100 g butter, at room temperature

2 tablespoons maple syrup

2 teaspoons instant coffee dissolved
in 1 tablespoon just-boiled water

200 g icing sugar, sifted

pecans, to decorate

*two 20-cm springform cake tins,
greased and bases lined with
greaseproof paper*

serves 8

Preheat the oven to 180°C (350°F) Gas 4.

Beat together the butter and sugar until pale and creamy, then beat
in the eggs, one at a time. Sift over the flour and fold in, then fold
in the coffee and pecans.

Divide the mixture between the prepared cake tins and spread
out in an even layer. Bake for about 20 minutes until golden and
a skewer inserted in the centre comes out clean.

Turn out on to a wire rack and leave to cool completely.

To make the frosting, beat the butter until creamy, then add the
maple syrup and coffee and sift over half the icing sugar. Beat
together until smooth and creamy, then gradually beat in the
remaining icing sugar.

Put one of the cakes on a serving plate and slice a thin layer off
the top to create a flat surface. Spread slightly less than half the
frosting over the top. Put the second cake on the filling and spread
the remaining frosting over the top. Decorate with whole pecans.

MOCHA FUDGE CAKE

This is the ultimate cake for hard-core mocha-holics. The bitter coffee takes the edge off the sweetness of the chocolate with a barely-there flavour. The outer crust bakes to a wonderfully crisp yet squidgy firmness, while the centre is meltingly soft. Serve with a fork – and thick cream if you're feeling particularly indulgent.

175 g butter

275 g dark chocolate, broken into pieces

250 g caster sugar

3 large eggs

100 g plain flour

2 tablespoons instant coffee dissolved in 2 tablespoons just-boiled water

icing sugar, to dust

thick cream, to serve (optional)

a 20-cm springform cake tin, greased and base lined with greaseproof paper

serves 8

Preheat the oven to 160°C (325°F) Gas 3.

Put the butter and chocolate in a heatproof bowl set over a pan of simmering water. Heat gently, stirring, until melted. Make sure the bowl does not touch the water. Remove from the heat and leave to cool for 5 minutes.

Stir in the sugar, then beat in the eggs, one at a time. Sift over the flour and fold in, then stir in the coffee.

Tip the mixture into the prepared cake tin and bake for 55 minutes until firm to the touch and pale and speckled on top. (There should be a slight wobble in the centre, but don't worry, the cake will firm up as it cools.) Remove from the oven and leave to cool in the tin.

To serve, carefully remove the cake from the tin and put on a serving plate. Dust with icing sugar and serve in wedges with thick cream, if desired.

DARK CHOCOLATE BROWNIES WITH COFFEE AND ARMAGNAC PRUNES

Nothing beats this heady combination of classic flavourings brought together in
these divinely squidgy, bitter-sweet chocolate brownies. Serve them as a mid-morning
or mid-afternoon treat, or enjoy them as dessert with a good scoop of vanilla ice cream.
The prunes need to be soaked overnight, so be sure to start the day before
you want to serve these brownies.

150 g pitted prunes

2 tablespoons Armagnac

60 ml freshly brewed espresso

85 g butter

175 g dark chocolate, broken
into pieces

175 g caster sugar

3 eggs

85 g plain flour

25 g cocoa powder

*a 20-cm square cake tin, lined
with greaseproof paper*

makes 16 brownies

Roughly chop the prunes into bite-sized pieces and put in
a bowl. Pour over the Armagnac and espresso, cover and leave
to soak overnight.

Preheat the oven to 180°C (350°F) Gas 4.

Put the butter and chocolate in a heatproof bowl set over a pan
of simmering water. Heat gently, stirring, until melted. Make sure
the bowl does not touch the water. Remove from the heat and
leave to cool for about 5 minutes.

Stir the sugar into the chocolate mixture, then beat in the eggs,
one at a time. Sift over the flour and cocoa powder and fold in,
then fold in the prunes and any remaining soaking liquid (there
should be less than a tablespoonful).

Pour the mixture into the prepared cake tin and bake for
20–25 minutes until firm to the touch and lightly speckled on
top. Leave to cool in the tin, then cut into 16 squares and serve.

COFFEE AND CINNAMON ROLLS

Warm, spicy cinnamon and smooth, rich coffee work in perfect harmony in these
sticky, sweet rolls. They're wonderful eaten warm, fresh from the oven, and
make the perfect choice for a leisurely brunch or afternoon snack.

400 g strong white bread flour

2 tablespoons caster sugar

½ teaspoon salt

2 teaspoons easy-blend dried yeast

3 eggs

80 ml lukewarm milk

50 g butter, melted

filling

115 g butter, at room temperature

115 g soft light brown sugar

1 tablespoon ground cinnamon

1½ tablespoons freshly
brewed espresso

glaze

40 g butter

1–2 tablespoons freshly
brewed espresso

140 g icing sugar, sifted

two large 6-hole muffin tins

makes 12 rolls

Sift the flour, sugar, salt and yeast into a large bowl, combine,
then make a well in the centre. Mix together the eggs, milk and
butter, then pour into the flour mixture and stir together.

Turn the dough out on to a floured surface and knead for
5–10 minutes, working in a little more flour if necessary, until
smooth and elastic. Put in a lightly greased bowl, grease the top
of the dough, cover in clingfilm and leave in a warm place for
about 1 hour until doubled in size.

Cut out twelve 15-cm squares of greaseproof paper and use to line
the muffin tins. To make the filling, beat together the butter, sugar,
cinnamon and espresso. Cover and chill for about 30 minutes.

Turn the dough out on to a floured surface and punch down, then
divide into two pieces. Roll out each piece to 20 x 26 cm. Spread
the filling over the dough and gently roll up from one long side to
form a roll. Slice each roll into six pieces and put in the lined
muffin cups. Wrap each muffin tin in a plastic bag and leave in a
warm place for 30 minutes until almost doubled in size.

Preheat the oven to 190°C (375°F) Gas 5. Bake the rolls for about
15 minutes until risen and golden, then transfer to a wire rack.

While the rolls cool, make the glaze. Put the butter and espresso in
a pan and heat gently until the butter has melted. Stir in the sugar
and heat gently, stirring, for about 3 minutes until smooth and
glossy and just bubbling. Bubble very gently for a further minute,
then spoon over the rolls. Serve warm.

BAKLAVA WITH RICH COFFEE SYRUP

Drenched in a sweet coffee syrup, sticky baklava are divine served with
a cup of black coffee. These are bite-sized ones and slightly less sweet
than traditional baklava – and all the more irresistible for it.

150 g pistachio nuts, finely chopped

150 g walnuts, finely chopped

1¼ teaspoons ground cinnamon

300 g filo pastry

85 g butter, melted

coffee syrup

225 g caster sugar

4 tablespoons freshly
brewed espresso

a 20-cm square cake tin, greased

makes about 25 baklava

Preheat the oven to 180°C (350°F) Gas 4. Combine the pistachio
nuts, walnuts and cinnamon and set aside.

Lay a sheet of filo pastry on a board, brush with melted butter and
use to line the prepared cake tin, butter-side down. Repeat with
another five layers of pastry, brushing the final one with butter.

Sprinkle the nut mixture over the pastry in an even layer, then fold
the excess pastry over the top. Top with another six layers of
buttered pastry and brush the top sheet with butter.

Using a sharp knife, cut the baklava into small squares or
diamonds, then bake for about 30 minutes until golden.

To make the coffee syrup, put the sugar and 125 ml water in a pan
and heat gently, stirring, until dissolved. Bring to the boil and keep
boiling rapidly for 4 minutes. Remove from the heat and set aside
to cool for about 10 minutes. Stir in the espresso.

Remove the baklava from the oven and spoon the syrup over the
top. Leave to cool completely before serving.

CREAMY COFFEE MILLEFEUILLES

These luscious, creamy pastries exploding with a rich coffee custard really are
an afternoon treat to sit down and linger over. Brew yourself a pot of coffee
and take half an hour out to relax and spoil yourself.

5 egg yolks

3½ tablespoons caster sugar

3½ tablespoons plain flour

300 ml single cream

200 ml milk

3½ teaspoons instant coffee
dissolved in 1½ tablespoons
just-boiled water

300 g puff pastry

icing sugar, to dust

two baking sheets, greased

makes 6 millefeuilles

Whisk the egg yolks, sugar and flour until combined and creamy.
Heat the cream and milk until hot but not boiling, then gradually
whisk in to the egg mixture until smooth. Stir in the coffee.

Return the mixture to the pan and heat very gently, stirring, for
5–10 minutes until you get a thick custard. Pour into a bowl,
press clingfilm on to the surface to prevent a skin forming and
leave to cool, then chill.

Preheat the oven to 200°C (400°F) Gas 6.

Roll out the puff pastry to about 5 mm thick and trim to a
18 x 30-cm rectangle. Cut into nine 6 x 10-cm rectangles,
arrange on the baking sheets and bake for about 12 minutes
until puffed up and golden. Transfer to a wire rack to cool.

To assemble, gently slice each pastry in half crossways using a
serrated knife to make 18 flat pastry slices. Arrange a piece of
pastry on each of six serving plates and spread each one with
about 3 tablespoons of the chilled coffee custard. Top each one
with another pastry slice and more coffee custard, then top with
the final pastry slices. Dust with icing sugar and serve.

indulgent desserts

HAZELNUT MERINGUES WITH COFFEE
AND WHITE CHOCOLATE CREAM

Toasting the hazelnuts really brings out their flavour in these fluffy, sticky, pale golden meringues. Sandwiched with a thick, luscious white coffee and chocolate cream, the combination of crisp, chewy and creamy is absolutely sublime.

60 g blanched hazelnuts

2 egg whites

115 g caster sugar

coffee and white chocolate cream

150 g white chocolate,
finely chopped

90 ml freshly brewed espresso

125 ml double cream

two baking sheets, lined with non-stick greaseproof paper

makes 6 pairs of meringues

To make the coffee and white chocolate cream, put the chocolate in a food processor, then pour over the espresso and blend until the chocolate is melted and thoroughly combined. Leave to cool.

Whip the cream until it stands in peaks, then fold in the coffee mixture. Cover and chill for at least 3–4 hours until thick.

Preheat the oven to 140°C (275°F) Gas 1.

Heat a non-stick frying pan, add the hazelnuts and stir over medium heat for about 3 minutes until toasted. Remove from the heat and chop finely. Set aside.

Put the egg whites in a clean, grease-free bowl and whisk until they form stiff peaks. Fold in the sugar, a couple of tablespoonfuls at a time, to make a thick, glossy meringue, then fold in the hazelnuts.

Spoon the mixture on to the prepared baking sheets to make 12 meringues, spacing them well apart, and bake for about 1 hour until crisp and dry.

Leave the meringues to cool on the baking sheets, then carefully peel off the greaseproof paper. To serve, sandwich the meringues together with the coffee and white chocolate cream.

WHITE CHOCOLATE AND KAHLÚA MOUSSE TORTE

This rich, indulgent dessert is something of a show-stopper. With a simple base made from crumbled brownies, and a filling of creamy, moussey white chocolate and coffee, it couldn't be easier to make. Use plain brownies, or ones studded with walnuts.

350 g dark chocolate brownies

200 g white chocolate, broken into pieces

100 ml freshly brewed espresso

2 tablespoons Kahlúa or other coffee liqueur

300 ml double cream

dark chocolate curls, to decorate

a 20-cm springform cake tin, base and sides lined with greaseproof paper

serves 8

Reserve about 250 g of the brownies and carefully cut the remainder into 7-mm thick slices, then use to line the sides of the prepared cake tin to a height of about 3.5 cm.

Crumble the remaining brownies into smallish chunks and scatter over the base of the tin. Using your fingers, press down gently to make a firm, flat base, then set aside.

Put the white chocolate in a heatproof bowl set over a pan of simmering water. Make sure the bowl does not touch the water. Heat gently, stirring, until melted. Remove from the heat and stir in the espresso until smooth and creamy, then stir in the Kahlúa. Leave to cool for about 10 minutes.

Whip the cream until it just stands in peaks, then fold in a couple of spoonfuls of the coffee mixture to loosen it. Continue folding in the coffee mixture a few spoonfuls at a time to make a smooth, creamy mixture. (If it becomes lumpy, break up the lumps very gently using a balloon whisk.)

Pour the mixture into the tin to fill the brownie case, then cover with clingfilm and chill overnight until set.

Remove the clingfilm, carefully release the torte from the tin and peel off the greaseproof paper. Serve decorated with dark chocolate curls and cut into slices.

COFFEE AND CHESTNUT ROULADE

Rich coffee custard, enriched with luscious chestnut purée and rolled up inside a light, golden sponge, then drizzled with a bitter-sweet mocha sauce, makes a wickedly indulgent dessert. As an alternative, you can sprinkle chopped *marrons glacés* (glazed chestnuts) over the custard in place of the chestnut purée.

4 eggs

115 g caster sugar, plus extra to sprinkle

115 g self-raising flour

85 g sweetened chestnut purée

coffee custard

3 egg yolks

2 tablespoons caster sugar

3 tablespoons plain flour

120 ml single cream

160 ml milk

2½ teaspoons instant coffee dissolved in 1 tablespoon boiling water

mocha sauce

85 g dark chocolate

90 ml freshly brewed espresso

180 ml double cream

a 33 x 23-cm Swiss roll tin, greased and lined with greaseproof paper

serves 6

To make the coffee custard, whisk together the egg yolks, sugar and flour until pale and creamy. Heat the cream and milk in a pan until hot but not boiling, then gradually whisk into the egg mixture. Return to the pan and heat very gently for 5–10 minutes, stirring, until you get a thick custard. Stir in the instant coffee, then pour into a bowl, press clingfilm on to the surface and leave to cool. Chill.

To make the mocha sauce, break the chocolate into pieces and put it in a pan with the espresso and cream. Heat gently, stirring, until smooth and creamy. Pour into a jug and leave to cool.

Preheat the oven to 220°C (425°F) Gas 7.

Put the eggs and sugar in a bowl and whisk for about 10 minutes until thick and pale and the whisk leaves a trail when lifted. Sift over about one-third of the flour and fold in, then repeat with the remaining thirds of flour. Pour into the prepared Swiss roll tin, tapping the edges so that it spreads out evenly, and bake for about 10 minutes, or until golden.

Lay a clean tea towel on the work surface, sprinkle with caster sugar and turn the cake on to it. Carefully peel off the lining paper, then roll the cake into a Swiss roll using the tea towel to help you. Leave to cool completely.

To assemble, carefully unroll the cake and spread the coffee custard over the surface, leaving a little space around the edges. Spoon over the chestnut purée, then carefully re-roll using the tea towel to support the cake. Serve in slices, drizzled with the mocha sauce.

CAPPUCCINO CHEESECAKE

Built on a mouth-watering biscuit base with a hint of dark, bitter chocolate, this smooth, creamy mascarpone cheesecake is topped with a layer of glossy white sour cream and dusted with cocoa, so that a slice really does resemble a cup of cappuccino.

150 g plain chocolate-covered digestive biscuits

60 g butter, melted

500 g mascarpone

125 ml crème fraîche

3 tablespoons instant coffee, dissolved in 3 tablespoons just-boiled water

125 g caster sugar, plus 1½ tablespoons for the topping

4 eggs, beaten

240 ml sour cream

cocoa powder, to dust

a 20-cm springform cake tin, greased

serves 8

Put the digestive biscuits in a food processor and process until they become crumbs, then combine with the melted butter. Tip the mixture into the prepared cake tin and smooth out to make an even base. Cover and chill for 30 minutes.

Preheat the oven to 180°C (350°F) Gas 4.

Beat together the mascarpone and crème fraîche until smooth, then stir in the coffee and sugar. Stir in the eggs until well mixed.

Wrap the base and sides of the tin in two single sheets of aluminium foil, then pour the mascarpone mixture over the crumb base. Put in a roasting tin and pour water around the cake tin so that it reaches half to two-thirds of the way up the sides. Bake for about 50 minutes until set but still soft.

Meanwhile, stir the remaining 1½ tablespoons sugar into the sour cream. Remove the cheesecake from the oven, gently spoon over the sour cream, spreading it out evenly, then return to the oven for 10 minutes.

Remove from the oven and leave to cool, then cover and chill for at least 4 hours or overnight. To serve, carefully unmould and dust with cocoa powder.

GROUND-COFFEE CRÊPES WITH
VANILLA ICE CREAM AND COFFEE SAUCE

Tuck into these light, crisp crêpes speckled with ground coffee beans, wrapped
around balls of vanilla ice cream and drenched in a rich, creamy coffee sauce.
The sauce can be served warm or cold.

2 tablespoons fine coffee grounds

115 g plain flour

1 tablespoon caster sugar

2 eggs, beaten

280 ml milk

sunflower oil, to grease

good-quality vanilla ice cream,
to serve

coffee sauce

120 ml double cream

3 tablespoons freshly
brewed espresso

150 g white chocolate,
roughly chopped

serves 4

Combine the coffee grounds, flour and sugar in a bowl, then make
a well in the centre. Beat in the eggs and about a quarter of the
milk to make a thick, smooth batter. Gradually beat in the
remaining milk, cover and leave to stand for 30 minutes.

To make the coffee sauce, put the cream, espresso and chocolate in
a pan and warm gently, stirring, until the chocolate has melted.
Keep warm or leave to cool, as desired.

Preheat the oven to its lowest setting.

To make the pancakes, heat a non-stick frying pan until very hot,
then moisten a piece of kitchen paper with sunflower oil and wipe
over the surface of the pan. Add a small ladleful of the batter and
swirl to thinly coat the base of the pan. Cook for about 1 minute
until the edges are dry and the crêpe golden underneath, then flip
over and cook the second side for 30 seconds or so until golden.
Keep warm in the oven while you make another seven crêpes.

Fold each crêpe in half, then into quarters to make a cone shape.
Place a ball of ice cream inside each cone. Drizzle with the coffee
sauce and serve.

COFFEE CRÈMES BRÛLÉES

What I really love about this dessert is the moment when you crack
through the crisp, glossy, burnt sugar crust and dig into the smooth, creamy,
coffee-flavoured custard below. A taste of sheer heaven.

500 ml single cream

5 teaspoons instant coffee granules

8 tablespoons caster sugar

4 egg yolks

2 tablespoons plain flour

1 tablespoon brandy

4 small ramekins

a kitchen blowtorch (optional)

serves 4

Put the cream, coffee granules and half the sugar in a pan and
warm gently until the coffee and sugar have dissolved, then
remove from the heat.

Put the egg yolks in a bowl and whisk in the flour to make a
smooth paste. Gradually whisk in the warm coffee cream mixture
until smooth, then return to the pan. Heat very gently, stirring,
for 5–10 minutes until you get a thick custard.

Stir in the brandy, then pour the custard into the ramekins. Leave
to cool, then cover and chill for at least 2 hours or overnight.

When you are ready to serve the crèmes brûlées, preheat the grill
to high. Sprinkle each one with 1 tablespoon of the remaining
sugar and place under the grill for about 5 minutes until the sugar
caramelizes. Remove from the heat, chill for a minute or two to
set the brûlée, then serve. (If you have a kitchen blowtorch, use
this instead of the grill to caramelize the sugar.)

RICH ALMOND TIRAMISÙ

Everyone loves this classic Italian dessert. Soft amaretti are used here instead of the traditional sponge fingers, but the distinctive taste of almond and kick of Kahlúa go wonderfully with the aromatic taste of coffee. If you can't find soft amaretti, you can use half the weight of crisp ones, although they don't absorb the coffee as well.

300 g mascarpone

3 tablespoons caster sugar

2 eggs, separated

300–350 g *amaretti morbidi* (soft amaretti)

120 ml cold espresso

about 1½ tablespoons Kahlúa

cocoa powder and finely grated chocolate, to sprinkle

4 serving dishes, preferably glass

serves 4

Put the mascarpone, sugar and egg yolks in a bowl and beat together until creamy.

In a clean, grease-free bowl, whisk the egg whites until they form stiff peaks. Fold a couple of spoonfuls of the egg whites into the mascarpone mixture, then fold in the remaining egg whites, one-third at a time.

Put a couple of spoonfuls of the mascarpone mixture into the base of four serving dishes and smooth the surface. Working carefully, soak about half the amaretti in the coffee for a minute or two until saturated (but not collapsing). Put a couple on top of the mascarpone, then sprinkle ¼–½ teaspoon Kahlúa over each serving.

Continue layering with more mascarpone, coffee-soaked amaretti and Kahlúa, finishing with a layer of mascarpone. Dust with cocoa powder, then cover and chill overnight.

To serve, sprinkle with more cocoa powder and grated chocolate.

STICKY COFFEE-TOFFEE PUDDING

This old-fashioned steamed pudding is a true winter warmer, delicious served with thick
cream or ice cream. What makes this pudding a real winner is the *dulce de leche*, a soft,
buttery toffee sauce from South America that can be found in most large supermarkets.
If you can't find it, make it by boiling an unopened tin of condensed milk in a pan of water
for 3 hours (being very careful not to let the pan boil dry), then leave to cool.

80 ml *dulce de leche*, plus extra to
serve (optional)

115 g butter, at room temperature

115 g caster sugar

2 eggs

115 g self-raising flour

1 tablespoon instant coffee dissolved
in 1 tablespoon boiling water

40 g walnut pieces

double cream or vanilla ice cream,
to serve

*six 150-ml individual pudding
moulds or one 1.2-litre pudding
basin, greased*

serves 6

Pour the *dulce de leche* into the bottom of the prepared pudding
moulds or basin.

Beat together the butter and sugar until pale and creamy, then
beat in the eggs, one at a time. Sift over the flour and fold in,
then stir in the coffee followed by the walnuts. Pour the mixture
into the moulds.

Cover each mould with 2 sheets of aluminium foil and tie firmly
in place with a piece of string.

Put the moulds in a large pan and pour boiling water into the pan
about two-thirds of the way up the sides of the moulds. Cover with
a lid and simmer gently for about 1½ hours, checking the water
level occasionally and topping up if necessary.

To serve, remove the foil, invert the moulds on to serving plates
and lift off. Serve with plenty of double cream or ice cream and
more *dulce de leche*, if desired.

DARK MOCHA AND KAHLÚA MOUSSE

Chocolate and coffee is a classic combination, and never better than in these
rich, dark, bitter chocolate mousses spiked with coffee liqueur. Although Kahlúa
is used here, any coffee liqueur or brandy will work well.

115 g dark chocolate, broken
into pieces

15 g butter, diced

2 eggs, separated

4 tablespoons double cream

3 tablespoons freshly
brewed espresso

1 tablespoon Kahlúa or other
coffee liqueur

dark chocolate curls, to serve
(optional)

serves 4

Put the chocolate in a heatproof bowl set over a pan of simmering
water. Make sure the bowl does not touch the water. Heat gently,
stirring, until melted. Remove from the heat and stir in the butter
until melted.

Beat the egg yolks into the chocolate mixture, then stir in the
cream followed by the espresso and Kahlúa.

In a clean, grease-free bowl, whisk the egg whites until they
stand in stiff peaks. Fold a couple of spoonfuls of egg white into
the chocolate mixture, then fold in the remaining egg whites
one-quarter at a time.

Spoon the mousse into four individual bowls, cover and chill
for at least 3 hours until set. Serve sprinkled with chocolate curls,
if desired.

PRALINE PROFITEROLES WITH STICKY COFFEE SAUCE

Nothing beats the pure indulgence of a plateful of these light choux buns filled with a praline cream and drenched in a rich, sticky coffee and white chocolate sauce.

115 g plain flour

90 ml milk

75 g butter, diced

3 eggs

coffee sauce

140 g white chocolate, broken into pieces

60 ml double cream

60 ml freshly brewed espresso

1 tablespoon Kahlúa or other coffee liqueur

praline cream

60 g caster sugar

60 g blanched hazelnuts

240 ml double cream

two baking sheets, lined with greaseproof paper

a piping bag (optional)

serves 4

To make the coffee sauce, put the chocolate, cream, espresso and Kahlúa in a pan and heat gently, stirring, until smooth and creamy. Pour into a jug and leave to cool, then cover and chill for 2–3 hours until thickened. (The longer you chill it, the thicker it will get.)

To make the praline, gently heat the sugar in a dry pan, stirring, for about 5 minutes until melted and golden. Add the hazelnuts and cook, stirring, for about 1 minute, then tip on to a sheet of greaseproof paper and leave to cool.

Preheat the oven to 220°C (425°F) Gas 7.

Sift the flour on to a sheet of greaseproof paper and set aside. Heat the milk, butter and 90 ml water in a pan and boil for 1 minute. Remove from the heat, shoot in the flour and stir until smooth.

Return to the heat, stirring constantly, for 1 minute, then remove from the heat. Beat in the eggs, one at a time, until smooth and glossy.

Drop neat spoonfuls of the mixture on to the baking sheets, spacing well apart, to make 12 buns. Bake for about 20 minutes until risen and crisp. Transfer to a wire rack, cut a slit in the side of each one to release the steam and leave to cool.

To serve, put the praline in a food processor and grind to a powder. Whip the cream and fold in the praline, then fill the profiteroles with the cream using a teaspoon or piping bag. Pour over the coffee sauce and serve.

ice creams, sorbets and drinks

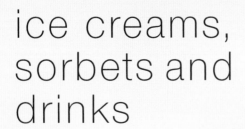

FROTHY ICED COFFEE

This light, frothy, refreshing blend is the perfect antidote to a hot summer's afternoon. For that extra kick, add a tablespoon of brandy or Kahlúa, or use a mixture of half cream and half milk.

240 ml crushed ice

120 ml milk

3 tablespoons freshly brewed espresso

1 tablespoon caster sugar

a scoop of good-quality vanilla ice cream

serves 1

Put the ice in a blender and pour over the milk, espresso and sugar.

Blend for about 30 seconds until frothy and slushy, then pour into a tall glass and top with a scoop of ice cream. Serve immediately.

CLASSIC COFFEE ICE CREAM

When faced with hundreds of flavours to choose from, a really classic coffee ice cream
is my first choice every time. Not too sweet, not too sickly, richly flavoured, aromatic,
rounded and just the right side of indulgent. Who could ask for more?

5 tablespoons ground coffee

240 ml just-boiled water

3 egg yolks

2 tablespoons plain flour

85 g caster sugar

160 ml single cream

120 ml milk

160 ml double cream

60 g chocolate-covered
coffee beans

an ice-cream maker

serves 4

Put the ground coffee in a cafetière. Pour the hot water over the
coffee and leave to brew for about 5 minutes before pressing down
the plunger. Leave to cool, then cover and chill.

Whisk together the egg yolks, flour and sugar until pale and
creamy. Heat the single cream and milk in a pan until hot but not
boiling, then gradually whisk into the egg mixture until smooth.

Return the mixture to the pan and heat very gently, stirring, for
5–10 minutes until you get a thick custard. Pour into a bowl, press
clingfilm on to the surface to prevent a skin forming and leave to
cool, then chill.

To make the ice cream, fold the double cream and coffee into the
chilled custard. Churn in an ice-cream maker until thick, then fold
in the coffee beans and freeze until firm.

❧

COFFEE-TOFFEE SWIRL

Creamy, slightly bitter coffee ice cream marbled with sinfully sweet *dulce de leche*
is the ultimate decadence. It suits both a sophisticated dinner party and a
lazy evening when what you crave is to curl up on the sofa and treat
yourself to a bowl of luxurious comfort food.

4 egg yolks

1 tablespoon cornflour

3 tablespoons caster sugar

300 ml milk

150 ml espresso, cooled

240 ml double cream

60 ml *dulce de leche* (see page 43)

an ice-cream maker

a freezerproof container

serves 6

Whisk together the egg yolks, cornflour and sugar until pale and creamy. Heat the milk in a pan until almost boiling, then gradually whisk into the egg mixture until smooth.

Return the mixture to the pan and heat very gently, stirring, for 5–10 minutes until you get a thick custard. Stir in the espresso, then pour into a bowl, press clingfilm on to the surface to prevent a skin forming and leave to cool, then chill.

To make the ice cream, fold the cream into the chilled custard. Churn in an ice-cream maker until thick (but not firm enough to scoop).

Spoon half the ice-cream mixture into a freezerproof container, then drizzle half the *dulce de leche* on top. Top with the rest of the ice cream and drizzle over the rest of the *dulce de leche*. Run the handle of a wooden spoon through the mixture 3–4 times to marble the mixture, then freeze for several hours until firm enough to scoop.

VANILLA AND WALNUT ICE CREAM
WITH A SHOT OF ESPRESSO

This fabulous concoction is the perfect way to end a meal – with dessert and coffee rolled into one. Serve the ice cream and coffee separately and allow your guests to combine them at the table. Some people like to pour the espresso over the ice cream, while others prefer to take a spoonful of ice cream and dip it into the coffee. Any leftover ice cream can be returned to the freezer for another time.

300 ml milk

1 vanilla pod

4 egg yolks

85 g caster sugar

1 tablespoon plain flour

300 ml double cream

60 g walnut pieces

4 shots of freshly brewed espresso, to serve

an ice-cream maker

serves 4

Pour the milk into a pan. Slit the vanilla pod lengthways and scrape the seeds into the pan, then add the vanilla pod itself. Bring to the boil, then remove from the heat and leave to stand for 15 minutes.

Whisk together the egg yolks, sugar and flour until pale and creamy. Remove the vanilla pod from the pan, then gradually whisk the milk into the egg mixture until smooth.

Return the mixture to the pan and heat very gently, stirring, for 5–10 minutes until you get a thick custard. Pour into a bowl, press a piece of clingfilm on to the surface to prevent a skin forming and leave to cool, then chill.

When chilled, stir the cream into the chilled custard, then churn in an ice-cream maker until thick and semi-frozen.

Meanwhile, preheat the oven to 190°C (375°F) Gas 5. Spread the walnuts on a baking sheet and bake for 3 minutes. Leave to cool, then fold into the thick, semi-frozen ice cream. Freeze until firm (follow the manufacturer's instructions for the ice-cream maker — the ice cream may have to be transferred to a freezerproof container for the last part of the freezing).

To serve, pour a shot of hot espresso into each of four bowls or teacups and top with a large scoop of ice cream.

ESPRESSO MARTINI

What could be better than combining a hit of caffeine with an ultra-sophisticated cocktail? This fabulous Martini offers just the right blend of sweetness, bitterness and refreshment, and makes the perfect choice when you need a reviving tonic with a dose of elegance. Try it with Kahlúa in place of the Frangelico if you prefer.

ice

3 tablespoons freshly brewed espresso

2 teaspoons caster sugar

2 tablespoons vodka

2 tablespoons Frangelico

a cocktail shaker

a cocktail glass

serves 1

Fill a cocktail shaker with ice. Pour over the espresso, then add the sugar, vodka and Frangelico. Wrap the cocktail shaker in a tea towel and shake well. Strain into a cocktail glass and serve.

COFFEE GRANITA

A granita falls somewhere between a sorbet and a slushy, iced coffee. It's deliciously refreshing in summer – either as a pick-me-up or as a light end to a meal. If you prefer yours a little sweeter, just add a little more sugar to the coffee.

4 tablespoons ground coffee

720 ml just-boiled water

75 g caster sugar

double cream, to serve (optional)

a large freezerproof container

serves 4

Put the ground coffee in a cafetière. Pour the hot water over the coffee and leave to brew for about 5 minutes before pressing down the plunger.

Pour the coffee into the container. (It should be no more than 2–3 cm deep.) Sprinkle over the sugar, stir until dissolved, then leave to cool.

Freeze for about 2 hours, or until the coffee starts to freeze around the outside of the container. Use a fork to break up the ice crystals, then freeze for a further 2 hours, breaking up the ice crystals every 30 minutes or so, until you have a thick, icy blend of fine ice crystals similar to snow. Spoon into tall glasses or dishes and serve on its own, or with double cream drizzled over the top.

❧

COFFEE AND VANILLA MILKSHAKE
WITH HOT CHOCOLATE SAUCE

This luxurious milkshake makes a wonderful summer refresher. The sauce thickens as it cools, so work quickly once you've made it – it should be the perfect drizzling consistency when you pour it into the milkshake.

3 tablespoons espresso, cooled

240 ml ice-cold milk

2–3 scoops of good-quality vanilla ice cream

hot chocolate sauce

1 tablespoon golden syrup

3 tablespoons double cream

2 teaspoons cocoa powder

serves 1

To make the hot chocolate sauce, put the golden syrup, cream and cocoa powder in a pan and heat gently, stirring, until the mixture just begins to bubble. Remove from the heat.

Put the espresso, milk and one scoop of the ice cream in a blender and blitz to combine. Pour the mixture into a tall glass, add one or two more scoops of ice cream and drizzle over the chocolate sauce. Serve immediately.

COFFEE AND NOUGAT PARFAIT

Parfaits are ideal for anyone who doesn't have an ice-cream maker. Made with a sugar syrup to give a thick, creamy custard, they can be frozen in moulds or dishes to make a soft, delectable ice. This one combining sweet, nutty nougat and bitter coffee is an irresistible combination.

115 g granulated sugar

4 egg yolks

120 ml freshly brewed espresso

240 ml double cream

100 g white nougat, chopped

sauce

100 g white chocolate, broken into pieces

60 ml freshly brewed espresso

four 175-ml dariole moulds or other suitable parfait moulds

serves 4

Put the sugar and 120 ml water in a pan and heat gently, stirring, until the sugar has dissolved. Bring to the boil and boil rapidly for about 7 minutes until the syrup reaches 115°C (239°F).

Put the egg yolks in a heatproof bowl and whisk until pale, then set over a pan of simmering water (making sure the bowl does not touch the water) and gradually whisk in the hot sugar syrup until creamy. Remove from the heat and continue whisking until cool and the whisk leaves a trail when lifted. Whisk in the espresso until frothy.

Whip the cream until it just holds in soft peaks. Fold a couple of spoonfuls of the coffee mixture into the cream to loosen it, then fold in the remaining coffee mixture.

Pour the mixture into the moulds, leaving a little space at the top. Cover and freeze for 1 hour.

Sprinkle the nougat over the top of the semi-frozen mixture, then top up with any remaining coffee mixture. Re-cover and freeze for a further 4 hours until firm.

To make the sauce, gently heat the chocolate and espresso over very low heat, stirring, until the mixture is smooth and creamy. Pour into a jug and leave to cool.

To serve, fill a bowl with hot water. Dip each mould into the water very briefly, then turn out on to a plate. Give the sauce a quick stir, then drizzle over and around the parfait and serve immediately.

CHOCOLATE, COFFEE AND VANILLA BOMBE

I've always loved ice-cream bombes, ever since childhood. My maternal grandmother used to make one for my birthday, and as such, they've always held a very special place in my heart. This recipe is for a single, large bombe, but you can just as easily use individual dariole moulds instead.

4 egg yolks

2 teaspoons cornflour

75 g caster sugar

300 ml milk

5 tablespoons freshly brewed espresso

1 teaspoon vanilla extract

300 ml whipping cream

100 g dark chocolate, broken into pieces

chocolate shavings, to serve

3 freezerproof containers

a 750-ml mould or pudding basin

serves 4–6

Whisk together the egg yolks, cornflour and sugar until smooth and creamy. Heat the milk in a pan until almost boiling, then gradually whisk into the egg mixture until smooth. Return to the pan and heat very gently, stirring, for 5–10 minutes until you get a thick custard. Pour into a bowl, press clingfilm on to the surface and leave to cool, then chill.

Divide the custard between three bowls. Stir the espresso into one and the vanilla extract into another. Whip the cream until thick and just holding in soft peaks, then fold one-third into the coffee custard and one-third into the vanilla custard.

Put the chocolate in a heatproof bowl set over a pan of simmering water. Make sure the bowl does not touch the water. Heat gently, stirring, until melted. Fold into the third bowl of custard. Fold in a little cream to loosen the mixture, then fold in the remaining cream.

Transfer the three custards into the individual freezerproof containers and freeze for about 1 hour until beginning to set around the sides. Blend each one in a food processor and return to the freezer for another 30 minutes.

Blend the chocolate ice cream, then scoop into the mould or basin and spread out in an even layer. Cover and freeze for a further hour, then blend the coffee ice cream and spread on top of the chocolate layer. Blend the vanilla ice cream, then gently spread on top. Re-cover and freeze overnight, or until firm.

To serve, dip the mould in hot water briefly, then turn out on to a serving plate. Decorate with chocolate shavings and serve in slices.

❦

COFFEE AND CARDAMOM KULFI

This classic Indian ice cream, made from slowly boiled milk, is most often found
flavoured with mango or pistachio. Here, however, it is flavoured with coffee and warmly
spiced cardamom – a sublime combination. Try to find traditional cone-shaped
kulfi moulds, but if you can't find them, dariole moulds will work just as well.

1.5 litres milk

10 cardamom pods

5 tablespoons freshly
brewed espresso

2 tablespoons caster sugar

toasted flaked almonds, to serve

an ice-cream maker

four kulfi or dariole moulds

serves 4

Put the milk in a pan and bring to simmering point (watching
carefully to ensure that it doesn't boil over), then reduce the heat
and simmer gently for about 30 minutes, stirring occasionally.

Put the cardamom pods in a mortar and crush lightly, then add
to the milk and simmer for a further 1½ hours until the milk has
reduced to about 420 ml. Strain into a jug and stir in the espresso
and sugar. Leave to cool, then cover and chill.

Churn the coffee mixture in an ice-cream maker until thick, then
spoon into the moulds, cover and freeze until firm.

To serve, briefly dip the moulds into boiling water, then turn out
on to serving plates and decorate with the almonds.

index